THE LIFE SCIENCE LIBRARY™

Interdependence
of Organisms and the
Environment

Isaac Nadeau

The Rosen Publishing Group's
PowerKids Press™
New York

For Wendell Berry

Published in 2006 by The Rosen Publishing Group, Inc.
29 East 21st Street, New York, NY 10010

First Edition

Editor: Rachel O'Connor
Book Design: Albert Hanner
Layout Design: Greg Tucker

Photo Credits: Cover, p. 7 (top) © William Manning/Corbis; p. 5 © David Muench/Corbis; p. 5 (top) © Gary Braasch/Corbis; p. 7 (bottom) © Galen Rowell/Corbis; p. 9 © Alexandra Michaels/Getty Images; p. 11 (top) © John Conrad/Corbis; p. 11 (bottom) © Arthur Morris/Corbis; p. 12 © PhotoDisc; p. 13 © Natalie Fobes/Corbis; p. 14 © Anthony Bannister/Corbis; p. 15 © Philippe Clement/naturepl.com; p. 17 (top) © Chase Swift/Corbis; p. 17 (bottom) © Paul A. Souders/Corbis; p. 19 © Florian Graner/naturepl.com; p. 21 © Charles E. Rotkin/Corbis; p. 22 © Bettmann/Corbis.

Library of Congress Cataloging-in-Publication Data

Nadeau, Isaac.
  Interdependence of organisms and the environment / Isaac Nadeau.— 1st ed.
      p. cm. — (The life science library)
  Includes index.
  ISBN 1-4042-2819-5 (library binding)
  1. Ecology—Juvenile literature. I. Title. II. Life science library (New York, N.Y.)
  QH541.14.N33 2006
  577—dc22
                              2005001748

Manufactured in the United States of America

Contents

What Is the Environment?

Every organism, or living thing, lives in an environment. An organism's environment includes everything that surrounds it. Air, water, sunlight, and soil are all part of the environment. The environment provides each organism with everything it needs to live.

All over Earth there are many different kinds of plants and animals that are specially suited to live in their environments. However, the environment can sometimes be harmful to the organisms that are part of it. No matter how different each environment is, they all have one thing in common. They are always changing. Plants and animals must react to these changes in order to **survive**.

Some environments are hot, some are cold, and some are dry. Others are made up mostly of water. Moolock Beach in Oregon is an example of a watery environment.

Desert environments, such as the one shown here in Arizona, are usually dry.

Organisms and the Environment

Ecology is concerned with the relationships between organisms and their environments. These relationships come in many forms. Many ecologists study the way in which animals and plants depend on one another for survival. For example, some flowers produce a sweet juice, called nectar, on which butterflies feed. When the butterflies fly away to other flowers, they carry the flowers' **pollen** with them. Flowers need pollen to form seeds, which become new flowers. You can see how butterflies and flowers depend on each other. Butterflies help flowers **reproduce**. Flowers provide butterflies with food.

Like butterflies, bees are drawn to flowers by their bright colors and strong smells. After the bee feeds off the flower, it flies off to another one, taking the flower's pollen with it.

Animals and plants have found ways to change with their environments. Many seals live in Antarctica, where snow and ice are part of their environment. In order to live in such a cold place, the seals' skin is thick and waterproof to keep them warm and dry.

Plants and the Environment

Plants depend on the Sun to survive. Without sunlight plants would not get the energy they need. They get this energy through photosynthesis. Photosynthesis occurs when the leaves of a plant get sunlight and **carbon dioxide** from the air. The sunlight and carbon dioxide are mixed with water from the soil to form sugars. Plants use these sugars as food. Plants then let **oxygen** out into the air through their leaves. For plants this oxygen is a waste product. For animals, including people, oxygen is important because it is in the air that we breathe. Plants are also a good supply of food for animals. In turn animals and people are important to plants because they let carbon dioxide out into the air.

Plants grow in all kinds of environments. Some plants, such as spruce trees, can live in cold environments. Their thin pine needles help them save water. This is important in a cold environment because the soil is often frozen, and there is little water during winter.

Animals and the Environment

Unlike plants, animals cannot produce their own food. Animals depend on plants and other animals for food. For example, a white-tailed deer eats the leaves and buds of many kinds of plants. Animals make use of plants for other things, too. For example, trees can provide homes for many animals and birds, including squirrels and owls.

Animals also depend on other animals for food. For example, wolves eat deer and bobcats eat mice. Animals also interact with the nonliving parts of their environments. Some birds swallow small rocks to help them break down their food. Others use the high rocky cliffs by the sea to lay their eggs. Snakes and turtles depend on the Sun to stay warm.

We call animals that eat plants herbivores. Giraffes are herbivores. Here you can see a giraffe enjoying his afternoon meal of leaves from a tree!

Animals that eat other animals are called carnivores. The great blue heron shown here is a carnivore. This bird feeds mainly on small fish.

Food Chains

A carrot is the root of a plant, and it has a lot of energy stored in it. When you eat a carrot, you are taking in energy that came from the Sun and the soil. You are also a link in a food chain.

When one living thing eats another living thing, they form what is called a food chain. For example, when a rabbit eats a plant, such as lettuce, that is a **link** in a food chain. When a fox eats the rabbit that has eaten the lettuce, that is another link in the chain. A final link occurs with what are known as decomposers, such as **fungi**. Decomposers help break down the bodies of dead animals and plants. This helps return the **nutrients** of the dead animals and plants to the soil. This in turn helps new plants grow, and the food chain starts all over again. There are many different food chains. Can you think of another one?

Decomposers, such as fungi, provide an important connection between the living and nonliving parts of an environment. They return nutrients to the soil, where plant roots can use them.

Working Together

Organisms can either work with each other or against each other. One way they work together is to make sure that each gets its share of food. For example, some **predators**, such as lions and wolves, work together to hunt animals that are larger or faster than they are. Certain plants have special fungi connected to their roots. These fungi help the plants get nitrogen, an important nutrient, from the soil. In return the plants provide the fungi with the sugars they need for food. Plants and animals can work against each other by struggling against one another for sunlight or food.

When wolves travel or hunt, they usually go in groups. These groups are called packs. The pack is usually made up of a family group and can consist of up to 15 members. Most packs, however, usually have about six members.

Changing over Time

The environment is always changing. One day might be warm, the next day might be cold. Plants and animals must be able to change with their environment. For example, when winter comes, many animals **hibernate** until spring. Changes also occur over long periods of time. For example, thousands of years ago, when Earth's **temperatures** were very cold, much of North America was covered in ice. This was during what is called an ice age. When Earth's temperatures warmed up, most of the ice disappeared. When changes happen in an environment, some organisms can **adapt** and survive, but others die. In some cases the changes can be so big that every member of a **species** dies. This is called extinction.

When winter comes many birds fly to warmer places. Birds use the Sun and the stars to help guide them.

Extinction occurs when an entire species dies out because it is unable to survive changes in the environment. Dinosaurs are a good example of animals that were not able to survive changes in their environment. Extinction has been occurring ever since life on Earth began.

Natural Selection

The process by which living things adapt over time to a changing environment is called evolution. Each member of a species is special, and each **evolves** in its own way. Two fish in the same species may look alike, but they are slightly different from one another. Sometimes these differences allow one fish to survive a change in the environment, while the other does not. For example, one fish might be able to survive slightly colder temperatures than the other. If the water becomes colder, the fish that survives is able to have babies, while the fish that dies is not. In most cases the babies will **inherit** the ability to survive colder temperatures. This is called natural selection.

Codfish are an example of fish that belong to the same species but are a little different from one another. Each cod adapts to fit its own special habitat. The cod shown here lives in the Barents Sea, which is part of the Arctic Ocean. The water can get very cold here. Other cod live in the Baltic Sea, which is in Northern Europe. The water here is warmer than the water in the Barents Sea. The Barents Sea cod would not be able to survive in the Baltic Sea, just as the Baltic Sea cod would die in the colder waters of the Barents Sea.

People and the Environment

People belong to the animal kingdom. As all animals do, people depend on their environments to stay alive. We eat plants and other animals. We use wood from trees to build our homes. Much of our clothing is made from plants, such as cotton from the cotton plant and linen from the flax plant. People can live in many different kinds of environments, ranging from cold mountains to hot deserts. One of the reasons we can do this is because we are able to change our environments to suit our needs. We use oil to heat our homes in winter. We grow and store food. More than any other species, people have changed the environments in which we live.

All over the world, trees in forests are being cut down. The wood is used to help people adapt to their environments. Wood is used to build homes and to make paper, among other things. Unfortunately, cutting down forests has an effect on the animals and plants that live there. When forests are cut down, many plants and animals die. Some animals must search for new places to live. It is important to remember that when we make changes to the environment, the effect may be helpful, harmful, or both.

Learning from Our Mistakes

When people change their environments, it has an effect on other species around them. Often the changes people make are not good for other species. Many plants and animals have become extinct because people have changed their environments too much, and others are close to dying out. This has been a problem in cities, where **urban development** has pushed out many animals and plants. As people learn more about the effects they have on other species, they are beginning to look for ways to prevent harm. People are learning how to protect the environment in ways that let other species live, too.

Glossary

adapt (uh-DAPT) To change to fit new conditions.

carbon dioxide (KAR-bin dy-OK-syd) A gas that plants take in from the air and use to make food.

evolves (ih-VOLVZ) Changes over many years.

fungi (FUN-jy) Living things that are like plants, but that do not have leaves, flowers, or green color, and that do not make their own food.

hibernate (HY-bur-nayt) To spend the winter in a sleeplike state.

inherit (in-HER-it) To receive something from a parent.

link (LINK) A connection between two things.

nutrients (NOO-tree-ints) Food that a living thing needs to live and grow.

oxygen (OK-sih-jen) A gas that has no color, taste, or odor and that is necessary for people and animals to breathe.

pollen (PAH-lin) A powder made by the male parts of flowers.

predators (PREH-duh-terz) Animals that kill other animals for food.

reproduce (ree-pruh-DOOS) To make more of something.

species (SPEE-sheez) A single kind of living thing. All people are one species.

survive (sur-VYV) To continue to exist.

temperatures (TEM-pruh-cherz) How hot or cold things are.

urban development (UR-bun dih-VEH-lup-munt) Major growth occurring in cities.

Index

Web Sites

Due to the changing nature of Internet links, PowerKids Press has developed an online list of Web sites related to the subject of this book. This site is updated regularly. Please use this link to access the list:
www.powerkidslinks.com/lsl/interdep/